100 SOLOS
FLUTE

100 SOLOS
FLUTE

HAL•LEONARD®
CORPORATION
7777 W. BLUEMOUND RD. P.O. BOX 13819 MILWAUKEE, WI 53213

WHERE HAVE ALL THE FLOWERS GONE?

Words and Music by Pete Seeger.

Moderately

WHEN THE SAINTS GO MARCHING IN.

Quick march

KUM BA YAH.

LOVE ME TENDER.

Words and Music by Elvis Presley and Vera Matson.

A DREAM IS A WISH YOUR HEART MAKES.

Words and Music by Mac David, Al Hoffman and Jerry Livingston.

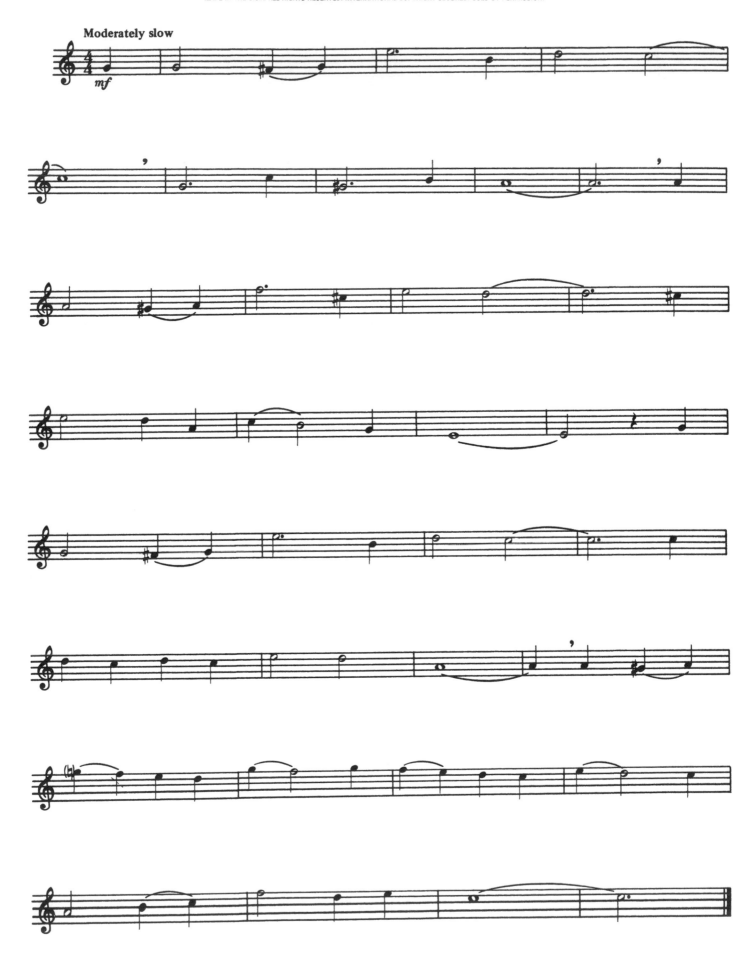

ALL MY LOVING.

Words and Music by John Lennon and Paul McCartney.

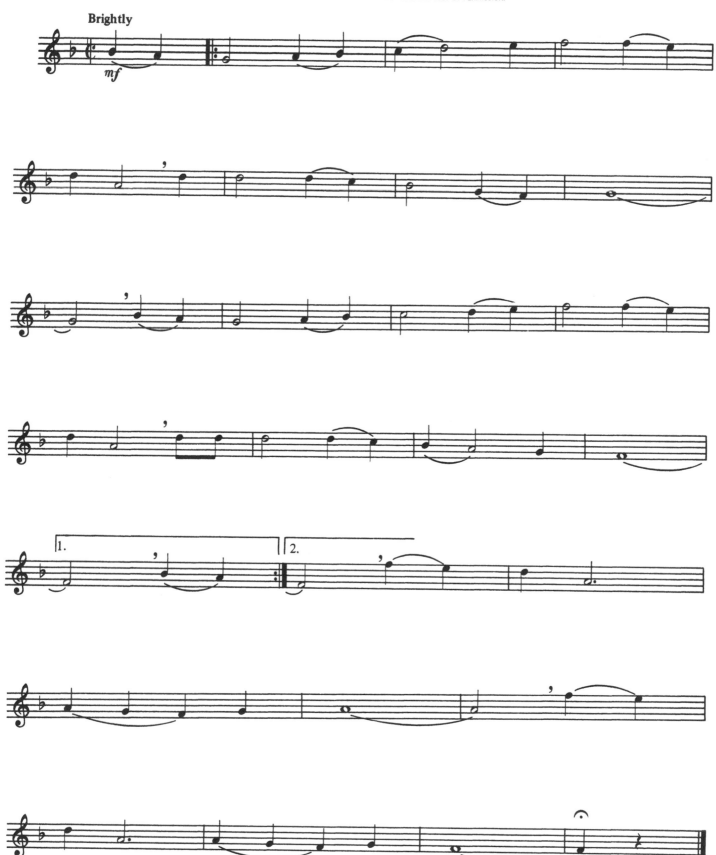

DO-RE-MI.
Words by Oscar Hammerstein II. Music by Richard Rodgers.

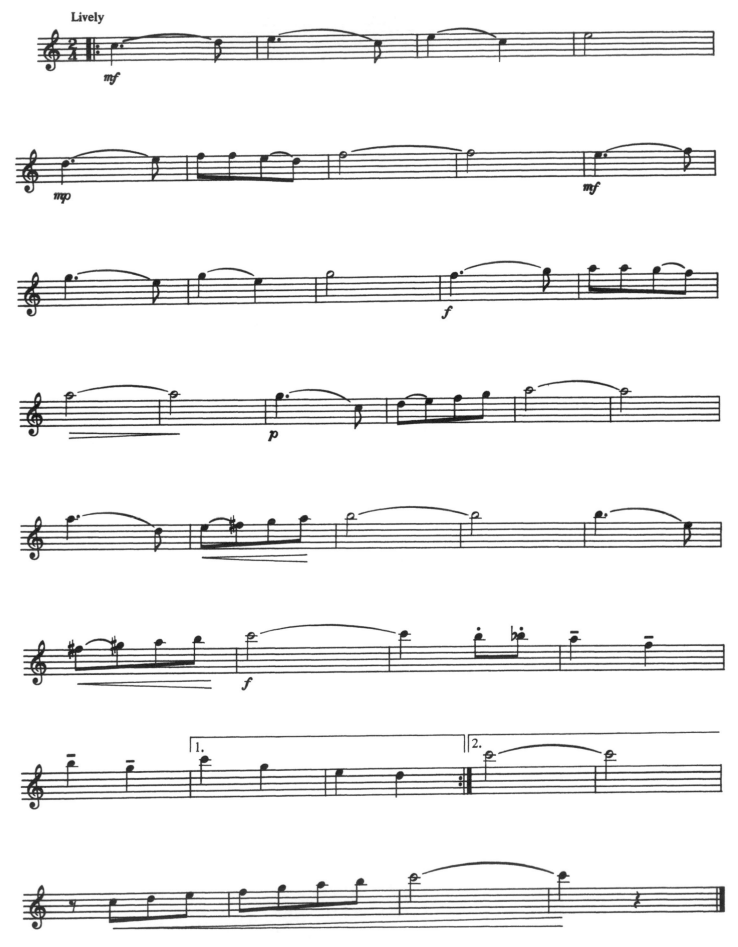

NEVER SMILE AT A CROCODILE.

Words by Jack Lawrence. Music by Frank Churchill.

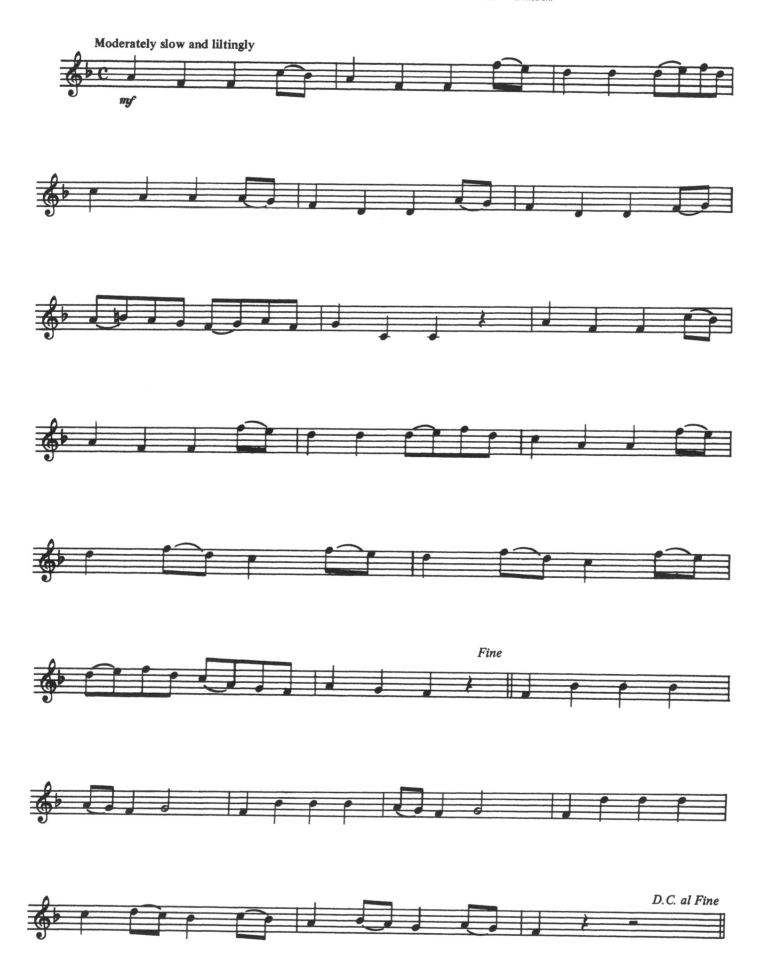

AS LONG AS HE NEEDS ME (FROM THE COLUMBIA PICTURE-ROMULUS FILM "OLIVER").

Words and Music by Lionel Bart.

NORWEGIAN WOOD.

Words and Music by John Lennon and Paul McCartney.

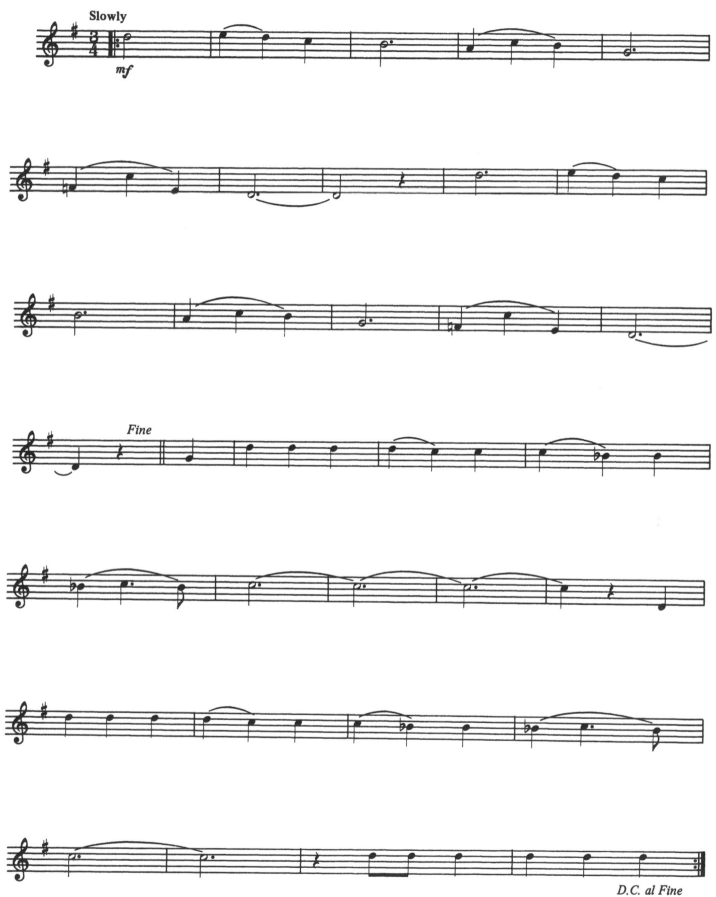

PICK A POCKET OR TWO (FROM THE COLUMBIA PICTURES-ROMULUS FILM "OLIVER").

Words and Music by Lionel Bart.

MORNING HAS BROKEN.

Words by Eleanor Farleon. Music (adaption) by Cat Stevens.

SCARBOROUGH FAIR.

Traditional.

Repeat 8va ad lib.

SMILE.

Words by John Turner, Geoffrey Parsons. Music by Charles Chaplin.

BIBBIDI-BOBBIDI-BOO.

Words by Jerry Livingston. Music by Mark David and Al Hoffman.

Light Schottische Tempo

COUNTRY GARDENS.
Traditional.

ROSES FROM THE SOUTH.
Johann Strauss.

THE BALLAD OF DAVY CROCKETT.

Words by Tom Blackburn. Music by George Bruns.

CIELITO LINDO.

Traditional.

I'LL BE YOUR SWEETHEART.

Words and Music by Harry Dacre.

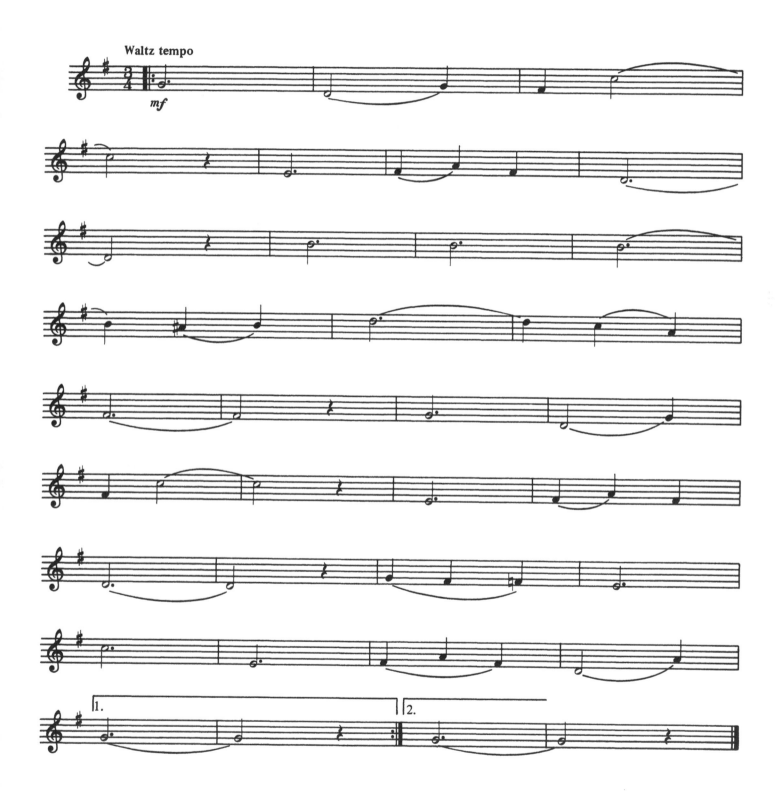

BRING ME SUNSHINE.

Words by Sylvia Dee. Music by Arthur Kent.

With an easy swing

SAILING.
Words and Music by Gavin Sutherland.

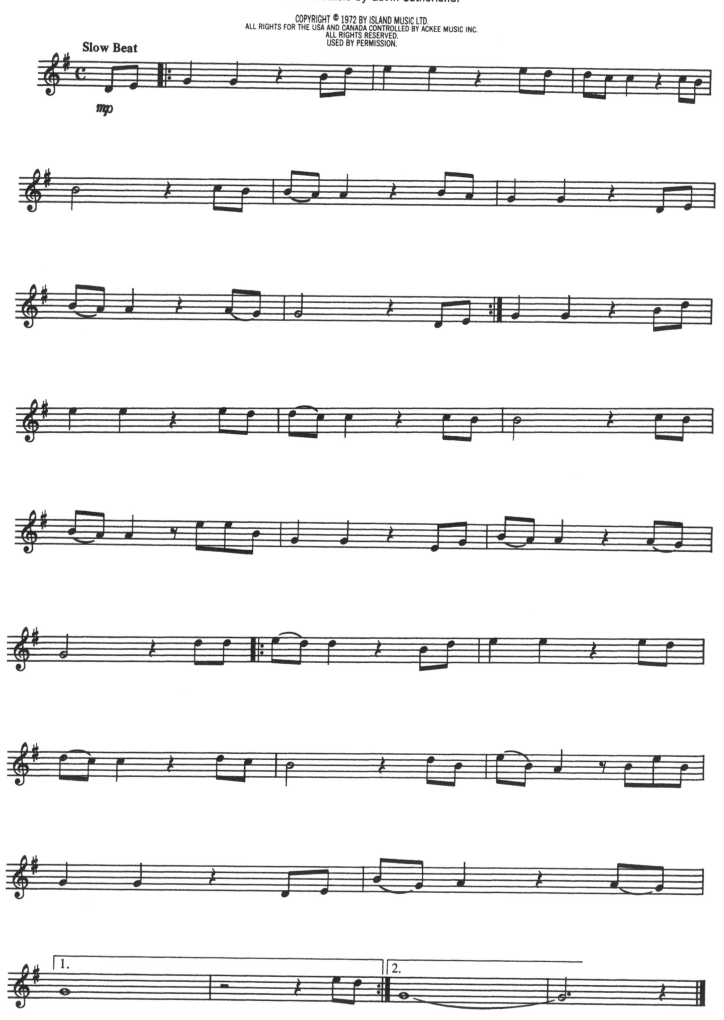

STREETS OF LONDON.

Words and Music by Ralph McTell.

A SPOONFUL OF SUGAR.

Words and Music by Richard M. Sherman and Robert B. Sherman.

AFTER THE BALL.

Words and Music by Charles K. Harris.

Moderately

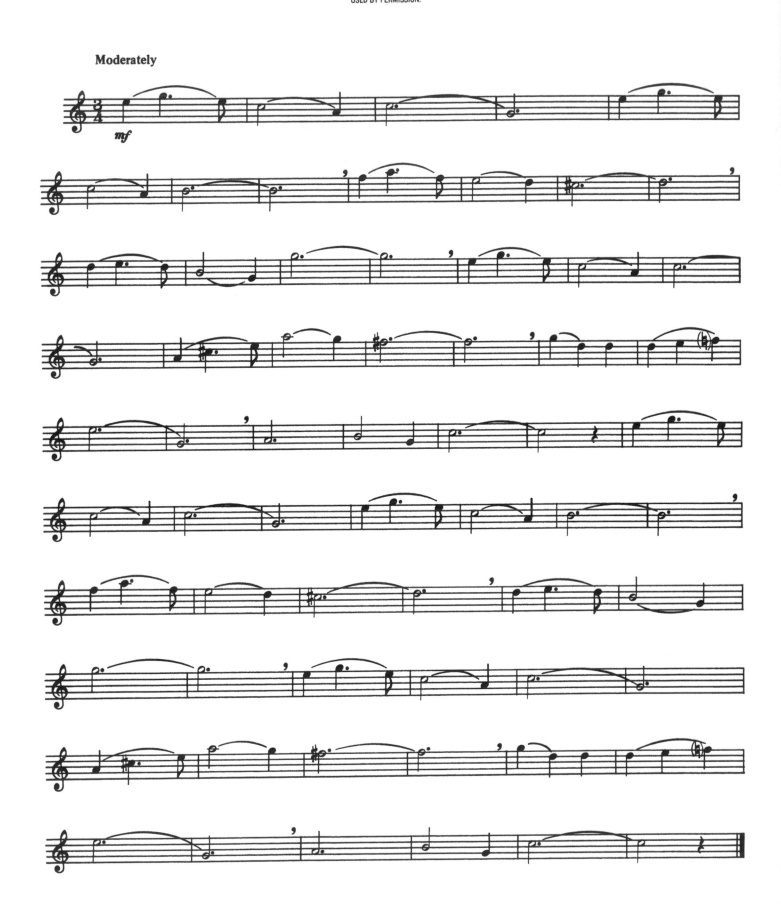

MY COLORING BOOK.

Words and Music by Fred Ebb and John Kander.

GIVE A LITTLE WHISTLE.

Words by Ned Washington. Music by Leigh Harline.

STRAWBERRY FIELDS FOREVER.
Words and Music by John Lennon and Paul McCartney.

STEPTOE AND SON.
Music by Ron Grainer.

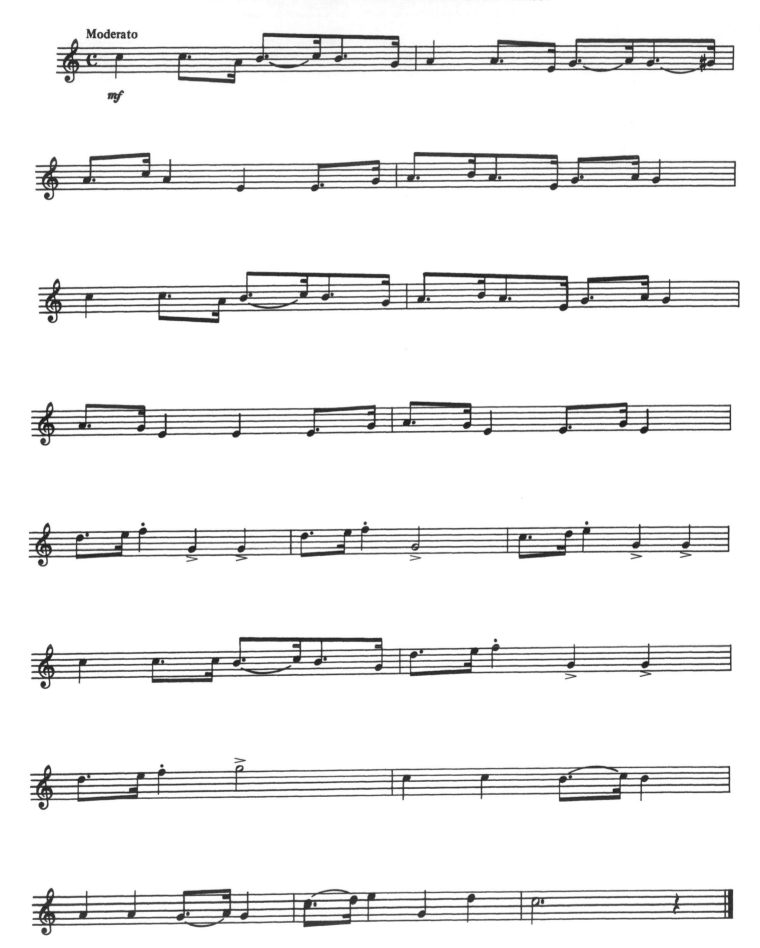

SHE'S LEAVING HOME.
Words and Music by John Lennon and Paul McCartney.

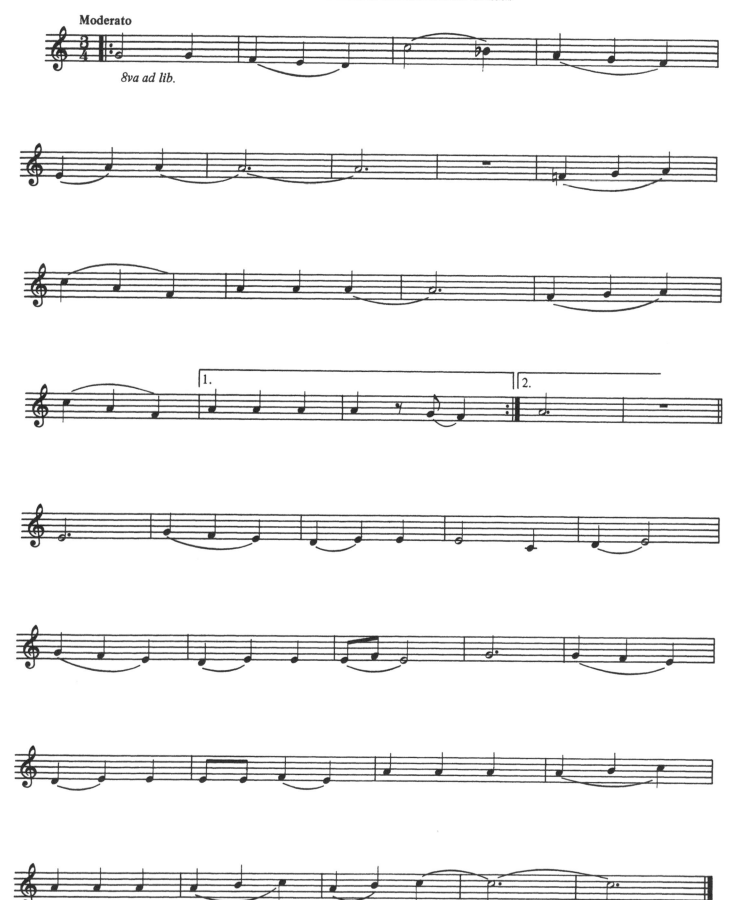

ANNIVERSARY SONG.

Words and Music by Al Jolson and Saul Chaplin.

YOUNGER THAN SPRINGTIME.

Words by Oscar Hammerstein. Music by Richard Rodgers.

BE BACK SOON (FROM THE COLUMBIA PICTURE-ROMULUS FILM "OLIVER").

Words and Music by Lionel Bart.

FIDDLER ON THE ROOF.

Words by Sheldon Harnick. Music by Jerry Bock.

HOW CAN I TELL YOU.

Words and Music by Cat Stevens.

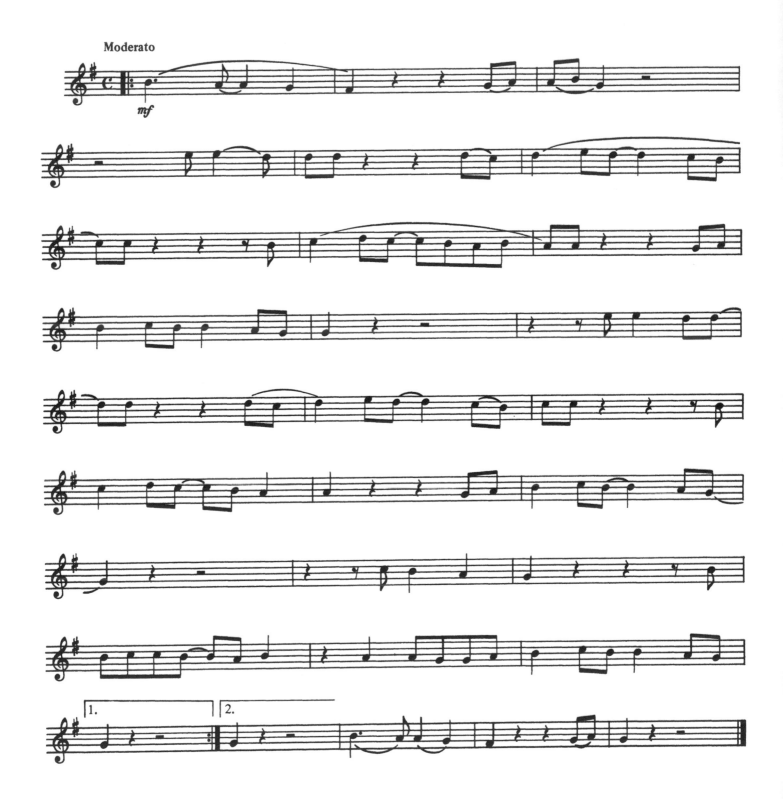

SUPERCALIFRAGILISTICEXPIALIDOCIOUS.
Words and Music by Richard M. Sherman and Robert B. Herman.

ON WINGS OF SONG.

Felix Mendelssohn.

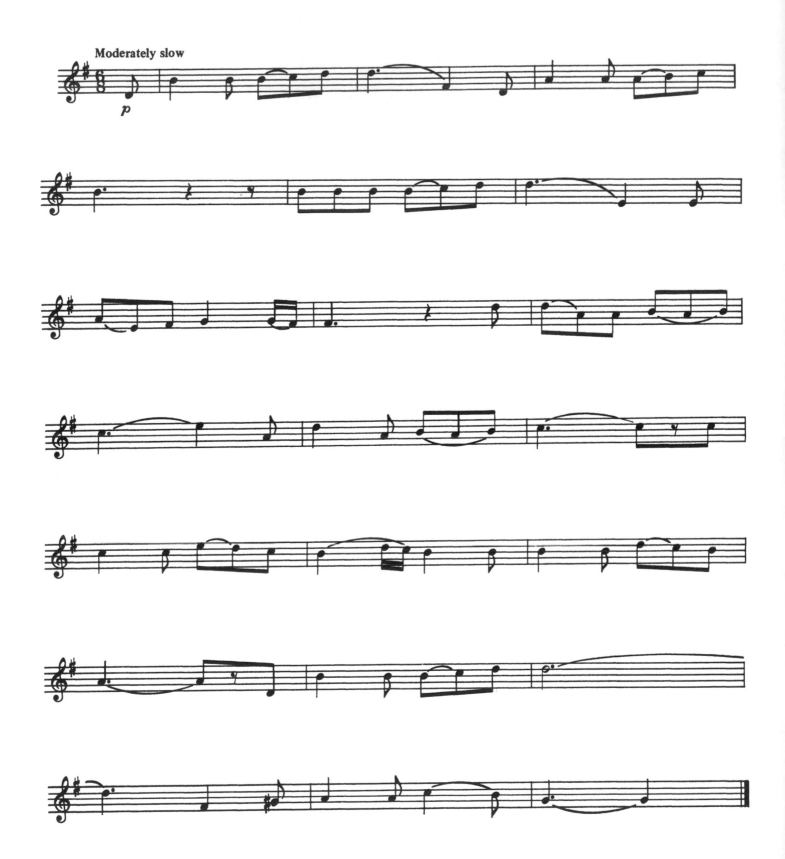

WHO DO YOU THINK YOU'RE KIDDING, MR. HITLER?

Words by Jimmy Perry. Music by Jimmy Perry and Derek Taverner.

FORTUOSITY.
Words and Music by Richard M. Sherman and Robert B. Sherman.

MICHELLE.
Words and Music by John Lennon and Paul McCartney.

LITTLE APRIL SHOWERS.

Words by Larry Morey. Music by Frank Churchill.

HELLO YOUNG LOVERS (FROM "THE KING AND I").

Words by Oscar Hammerstein. Music by Richard Rodgers.

WHEN A FELON'S NOT ENGAGED IN HIS EMPLOYMENT.

Words by W.S. Gilbert. Music by Arthur Sullivan.

GREENSLEEVES.
Traditional.

Moderately

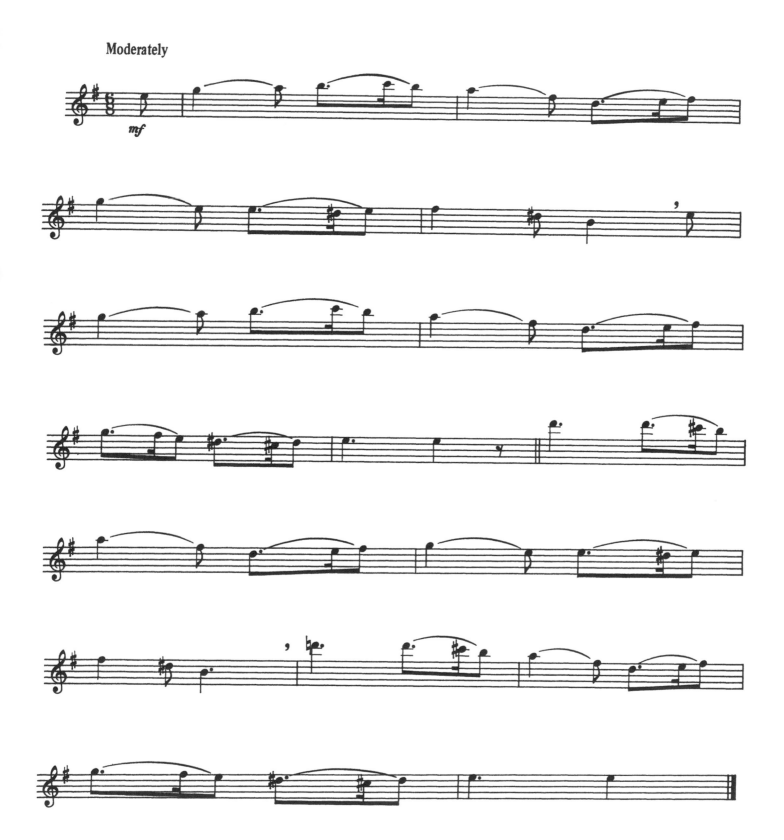

SWING LOW SWEET CHARIOT.

SERENADE.
Schubert.

SHALL WE DANCE (FROM THE KING AND I).

Words by Oscar Hammerstein. Music by Richard Rodgers.

ROMANCE IN G.

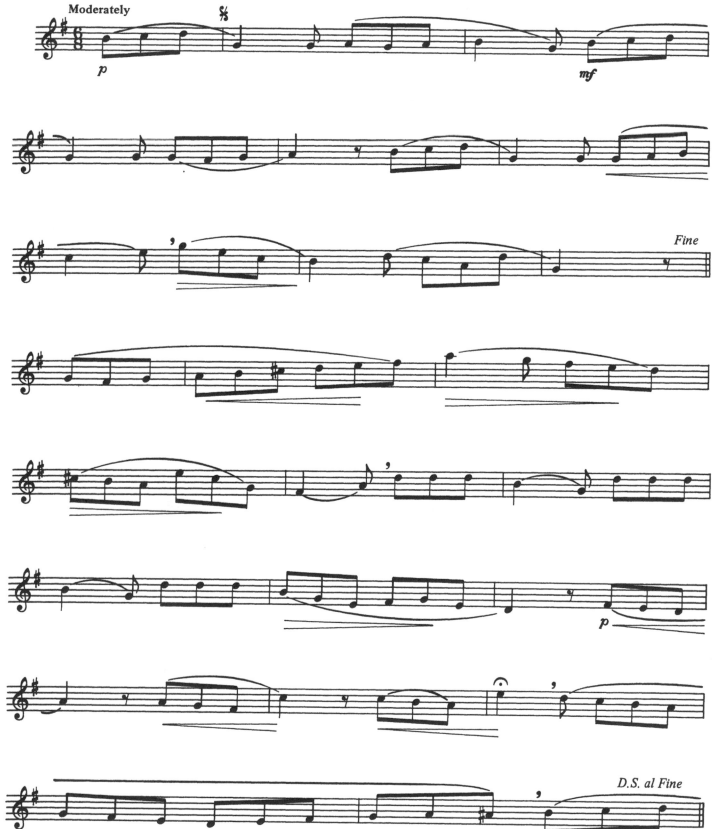

WHERE IS LOVE (FROM THE COLUMBIA PICTURES-ROMULUS FILM "OLIVER").

Words and Music by Lionel Bart.

WHEN I'M SIXTY FOUR.

Words and Music by John Lennon and Paul McCartney.

PRELUDE IN G MAJOR.

Chopin.

PRELUDE IN D MINOR.

Chopin.

WHO WILL BUY? (FROM THE COLUMBIA PICTURES-ROMULUS FILM "OLIVER!").

Words and Music by Lionel Bart.

CHIM CHIM CHER-EE.

Words and Music by Richard M. Sherman and Robert B. Sherman.

REVIEWING THE SITUATION (FROM THE COLUMBIA PICTURES-ROMULUS FILM "OLIVER").

Words and Music by Lionel Bart.

I DON'T KNOW HOW TO LOVE HIM.

Words by Tim Rice. Music by Andrew Lloyd Webber.

LITTLE BOXES.

By Malvina Reynolds.

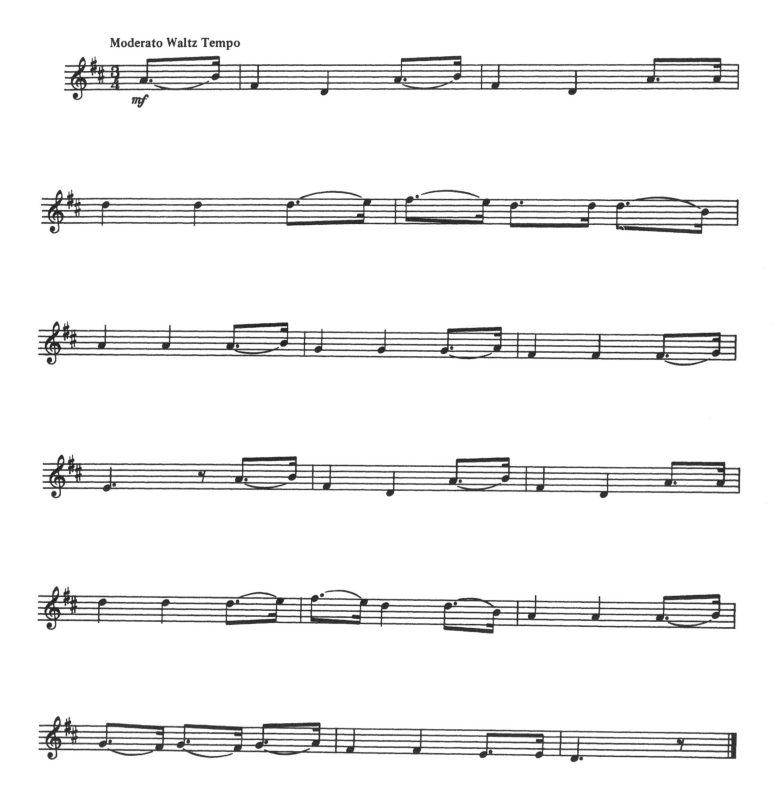

LA CI DAREM LA MANO.

W.A. Mozart.

NOCTURNE (BORODIN).

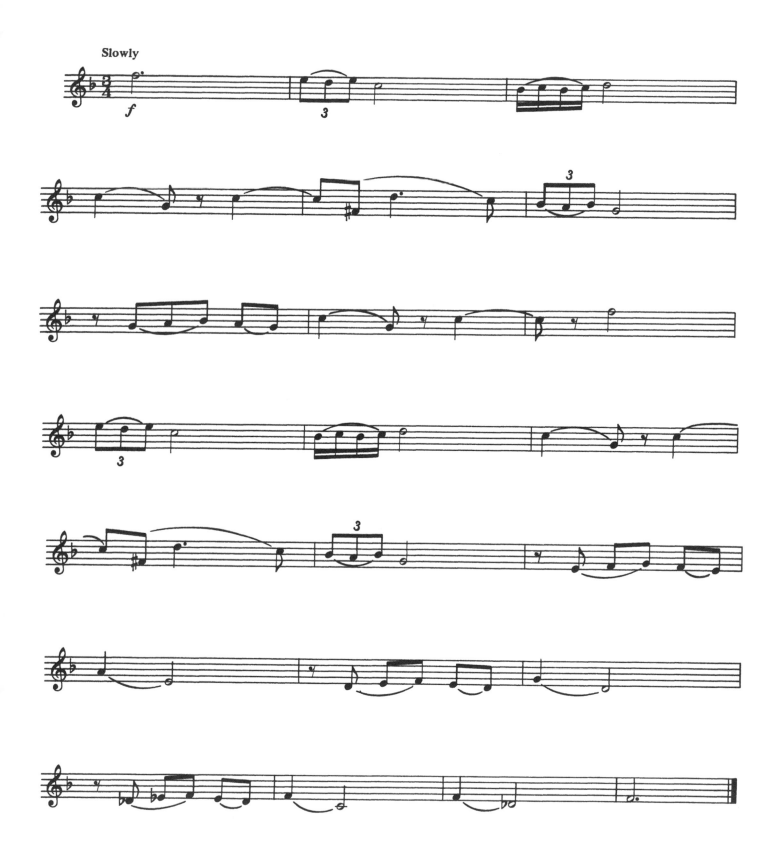

FOOD GLORIOUS FOOD (FROM THE COLUMBIA PICTURE-ROMULUS FILM "OLIVER").

Words and Music by Lionel Bart.

KARMA CHAMELEON.

Words and Music by Phil Pickett, George O'Dowd, Jon Moss, Mickey Craig & Roy Hay.

BALLADE POUR ADELINE.

Music by Paul de Senneville.

MARIA.
Words by Oscar Hammerstein II. Music by Richard Rodgers.

OOM PAH PAH (FROM THE COLUMBIA PICTURES-ROMULUS FILM "OLIVER").

Words and Music by Lionel Bart.

YELLOW SUBMARINE.

Words and Music by John Lennon and Paul McCartney.

CONSIDER YOURSELF (FROM THE COLUMBIA PICTURE-ROMULUS FILM "OLIVER").

Words and Music by Lionel Bart.

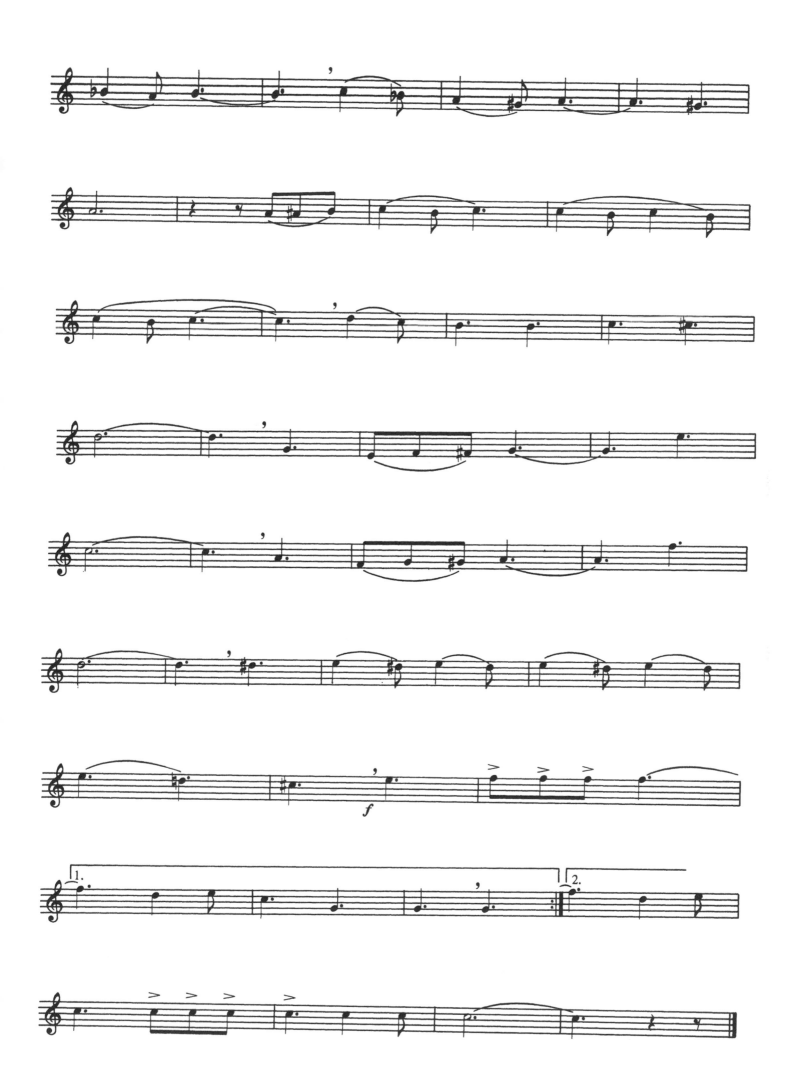

WATERLOO.

Words and Music by Benny Andersson, Stig Anderson and Bjorn Ulvaeus.

PENNY LANE.

Words and Music by John Lennon and Paul McCartney.

LULLABY OF BIRDLAND.
Words by George David Weiss. Music by George Shearing.

CAROLINA MOON.

Words by Benny Davis. Music by Joe Burke.

SCOTTISH DANCE.

Beethoven.

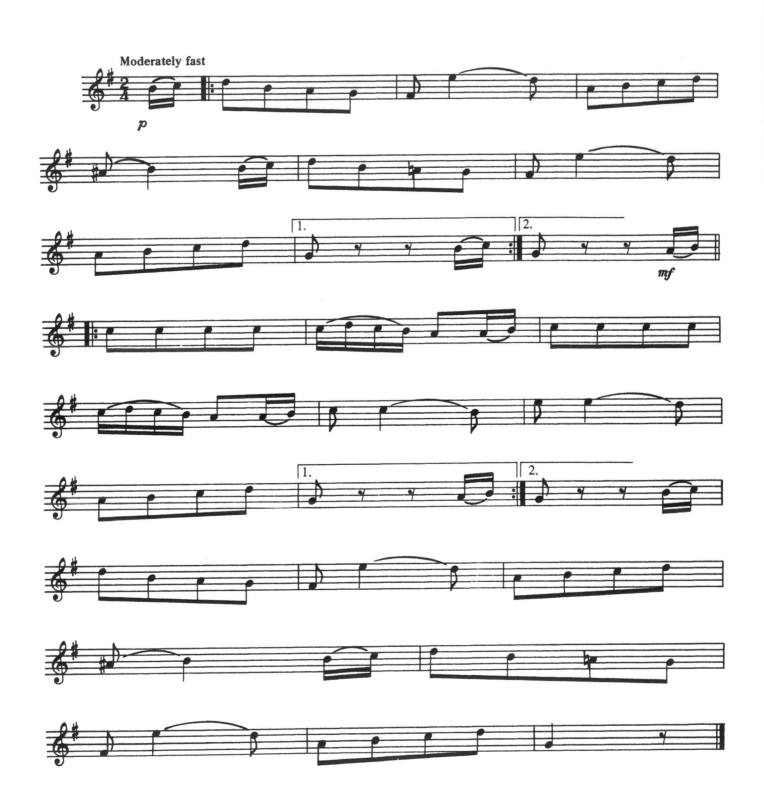

RADETZKY MARCH.

Johann Strauss.

WITH A LITTLE HELP FROM MY FRIENDS.

Words and Music by John Lennon & Paul McCartney.

THE ENTERTAINER.
Scott Joplin.

AH, SO PURE (MARTHA).

von Flotow.

AMERICAN PATROL.

F.W. Meacham.

BATTLE HYMN OF THE REPUBLIC.

Julia Ward Howe.

BARCAROLLE.

J. Offenbach.

CHANSON TRISTE.

Tchaikovsky.

Allegro non troppo

FANTASIE IMPROMPTU.

Frederic Chopin.

FÜR ELISE.

Beethoven.

GAVOTTE.

Gossec.

AMERICA, THE BEAUTIFUL.

Samuel A. Ward.

HATIKVOH (THE HOPE).

Hebrew National Anthem.

IRISH WASHERWOMAN.

Traditional.

ARKANSAS TRAVELLER.

Traditional.

POP GOES THE WEASEL.

Traditional.

LA CUMPARSITA.

G.H. Matos Rodriquez.

LA DONNA E MOBILE.

Verdi.

LA SPAGNOLA.

Vincenzo Di Chiara.

Tempo di Valse

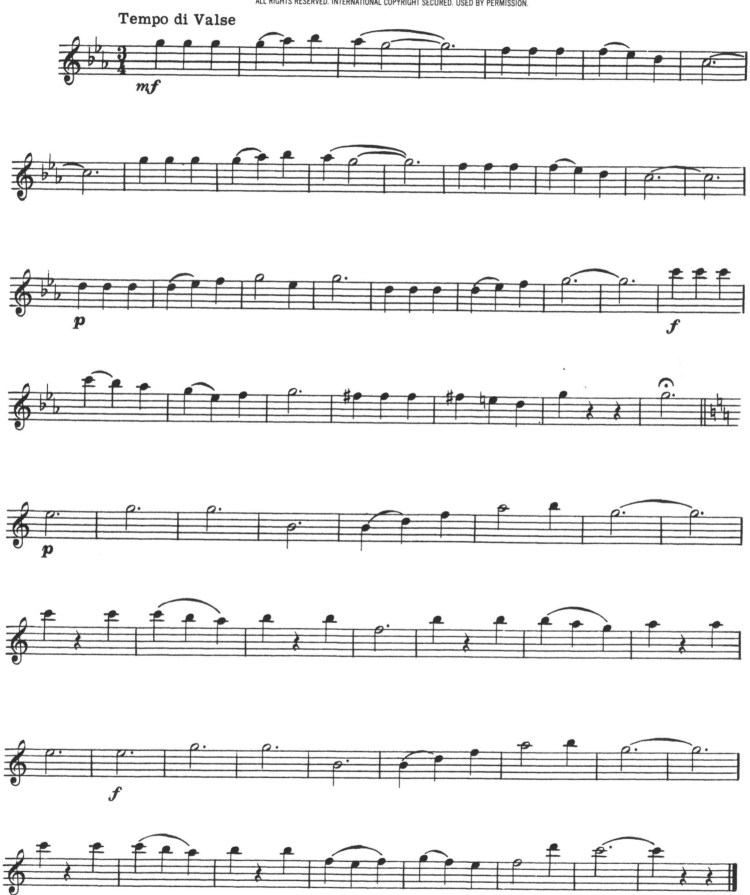

LE CYGNE.

Saint-Saens.

MINUET IN G.

Beethoven.

POMP AND CIRCUMSTANCE.

Edward Elgar.

MIGHTY LAK' A ROSE.

Ethelbert Nevin.

NONE BUT THE LONELY HEART.

Tchaikovsky.

I DREAMT THAT I DWELT IN MARBLE HALLS.

M. Balfe.

REVERIE.
Claude Debussy.

SERENADE.

Franz Josef Haydn.

TO A WILD ROSE.

Edward MacDowell.

WALTZ.

Brahms.